surfing

surfing

MW00783849

waterskiing

snorkeling

waterskiing

2

sculling

waterskiing

waterskiing

3

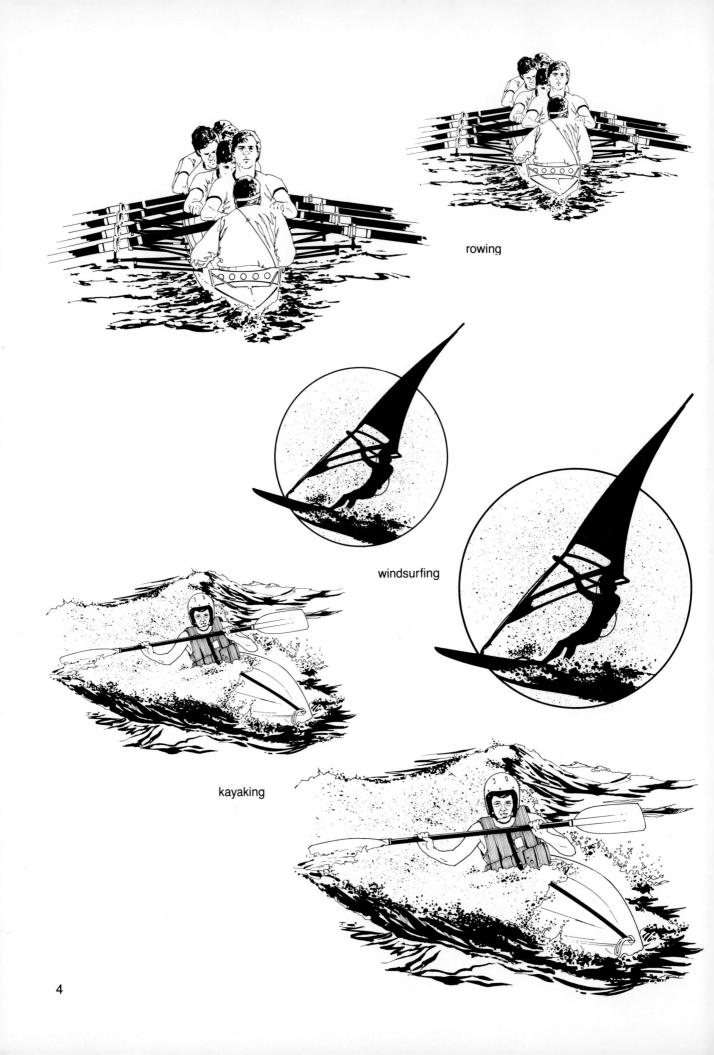

rowing

windsurfing

kayaking

4

jet skiing

powerboat racing

jet boating

5

diving

windsurfing

yachting

6

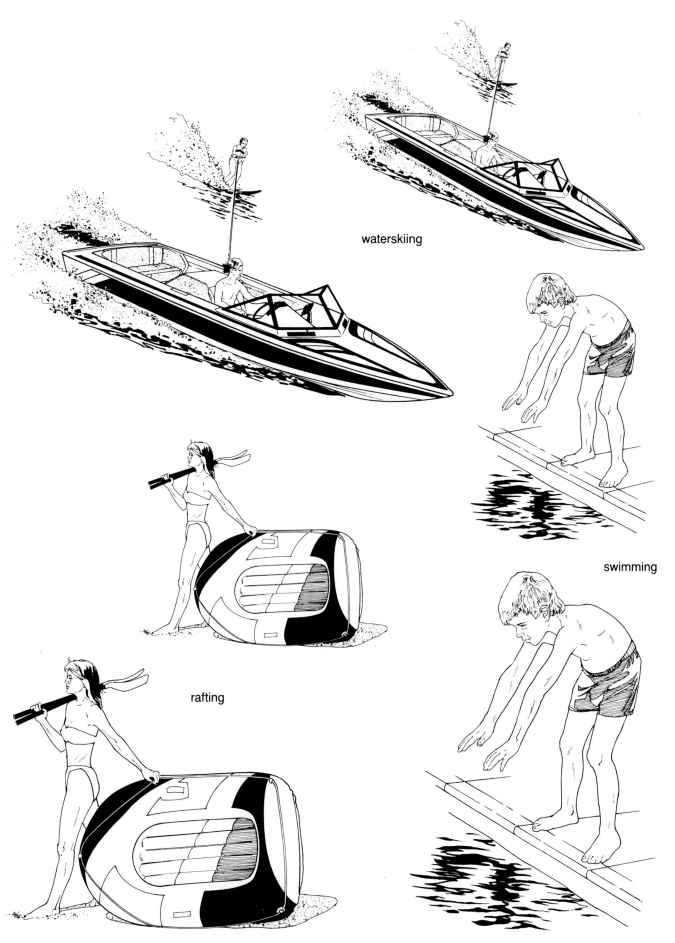

waterskiing

swimming

rafting

7

scuba diving

scuba diving

sculling

skin diving

windsurfing

diving

9

parasailing

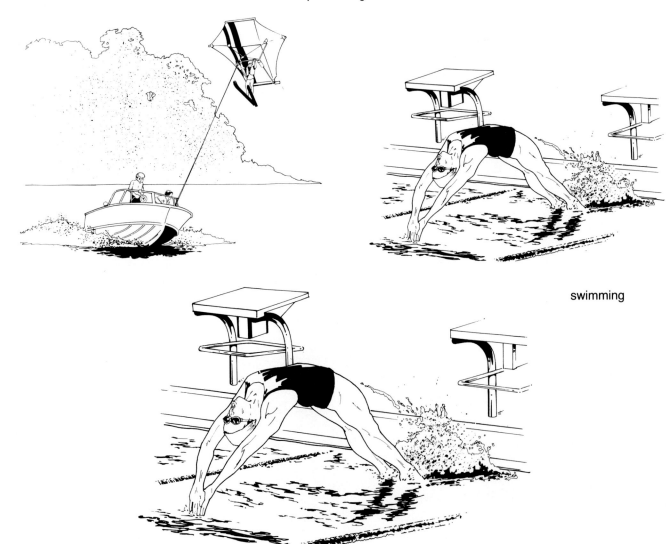

swimming

surfing

rafting

catamaran sailing

sailing

canoeing

swimming

catamaran sailing

13

swimming

diving

kayaking

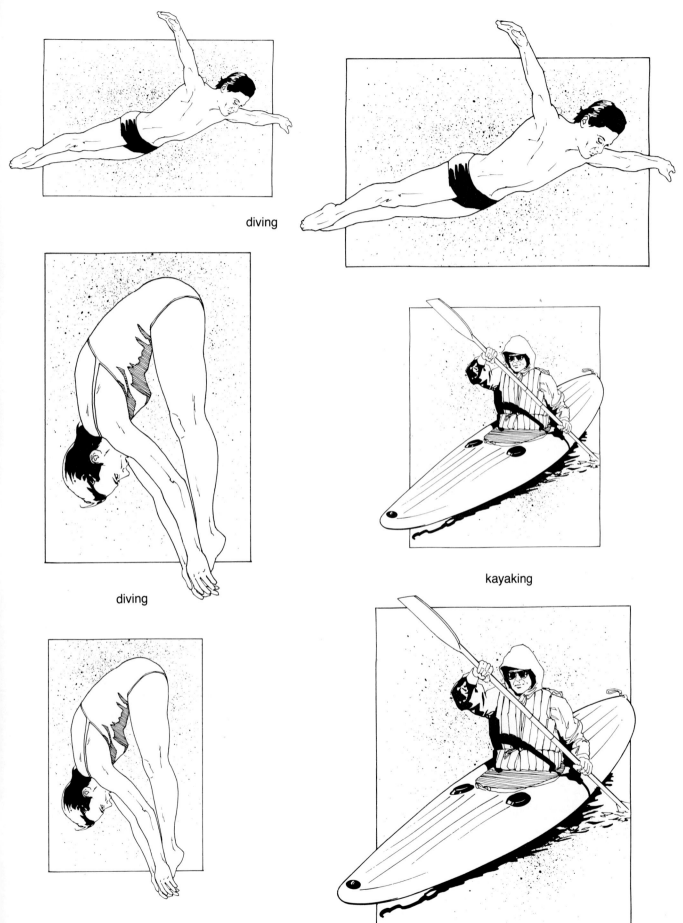

diving

diving

kayaking

scuba diving

swimming

scuba diving

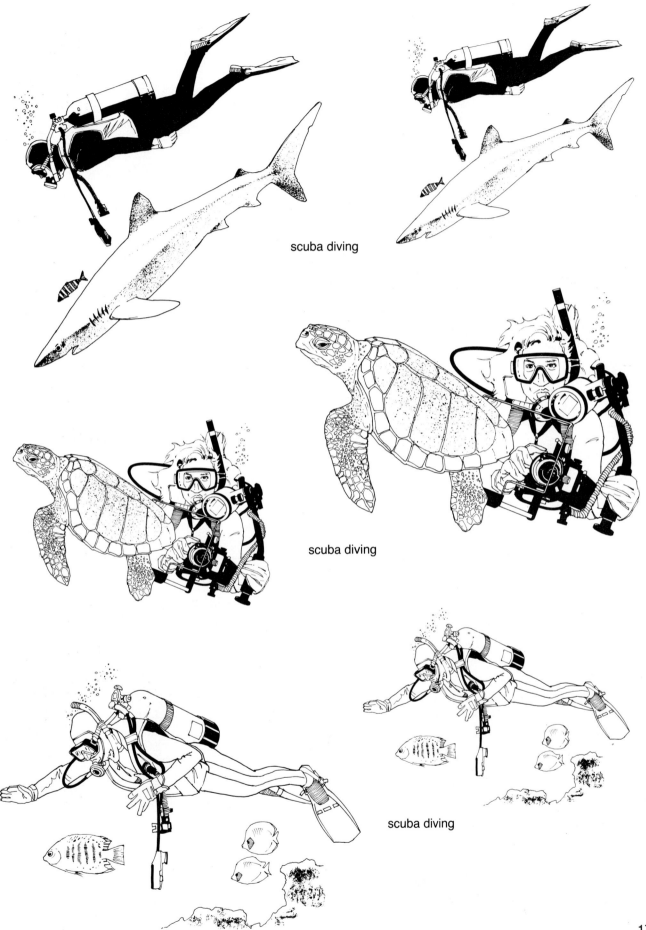

scuba diving

scuba diving

scuba diving

water polo

diving

swimming

water polo

swimming

swimming

19

canoeing

diving

motorboating

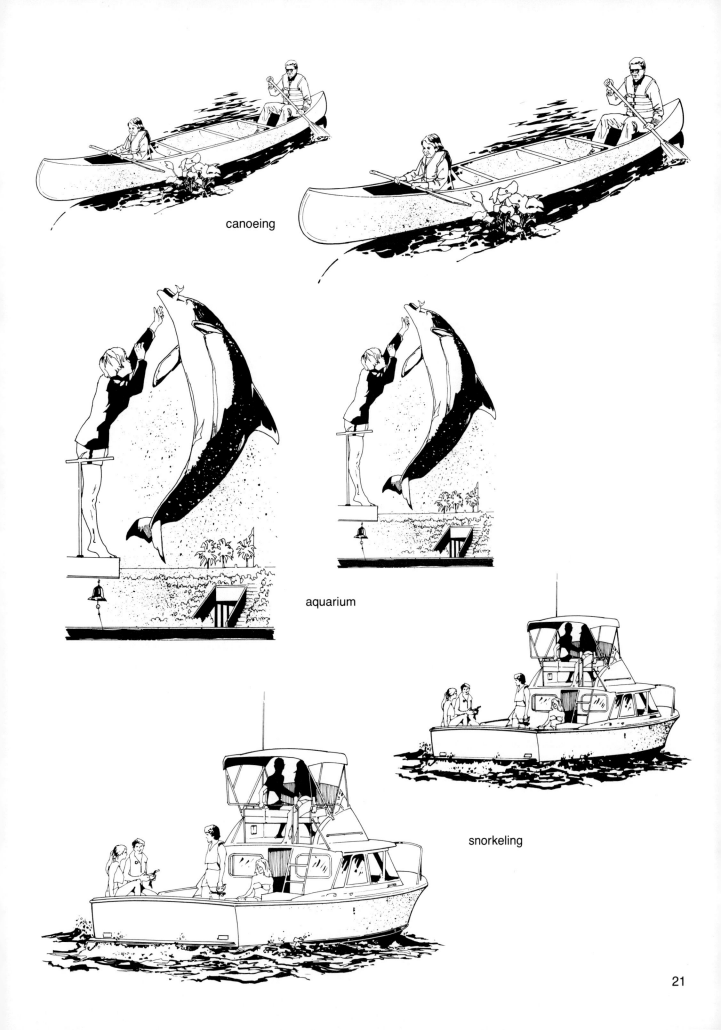

canoeing

aquarium

snorkeling

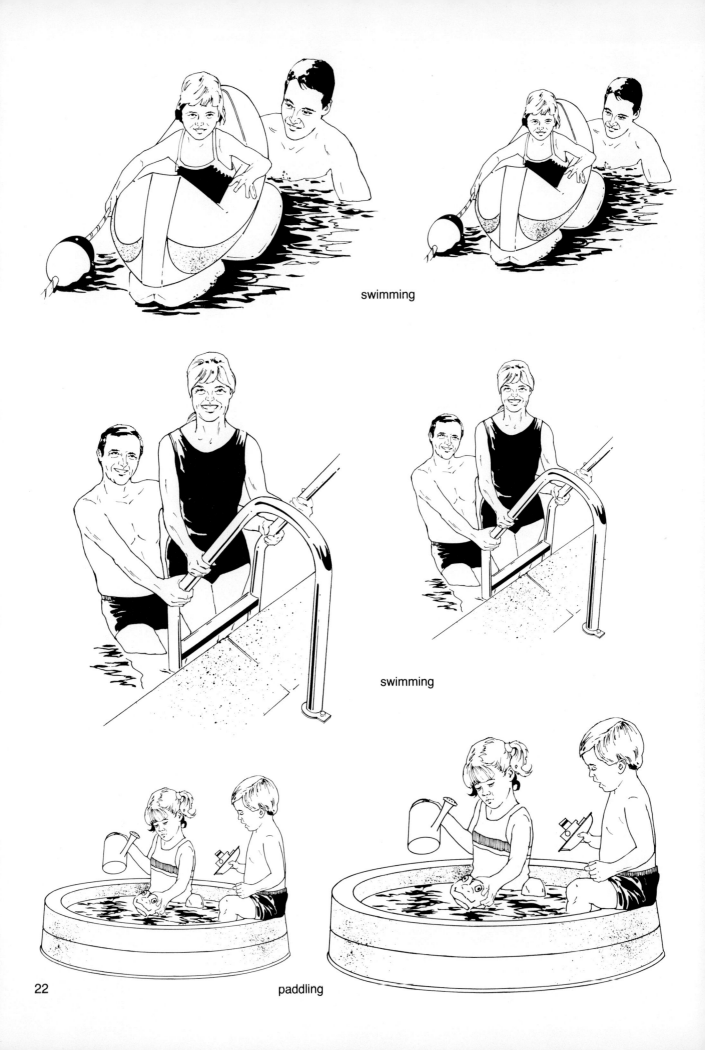

swimming

swimming

22

paddling

swimming

swimming

paddling

kayaking

windsurfing

paddleboating

24

motorboating

rafting

rafting

floating

waterskiing

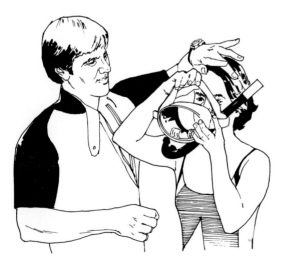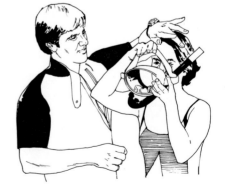

snorkeling

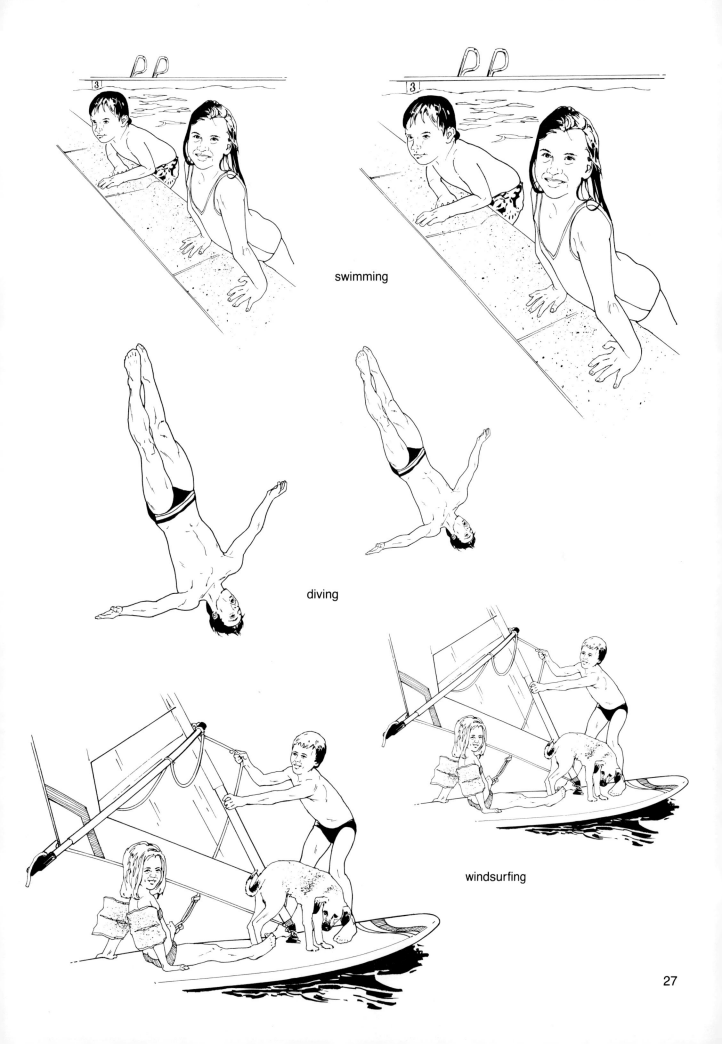

swimming

diving

windsurfing

27

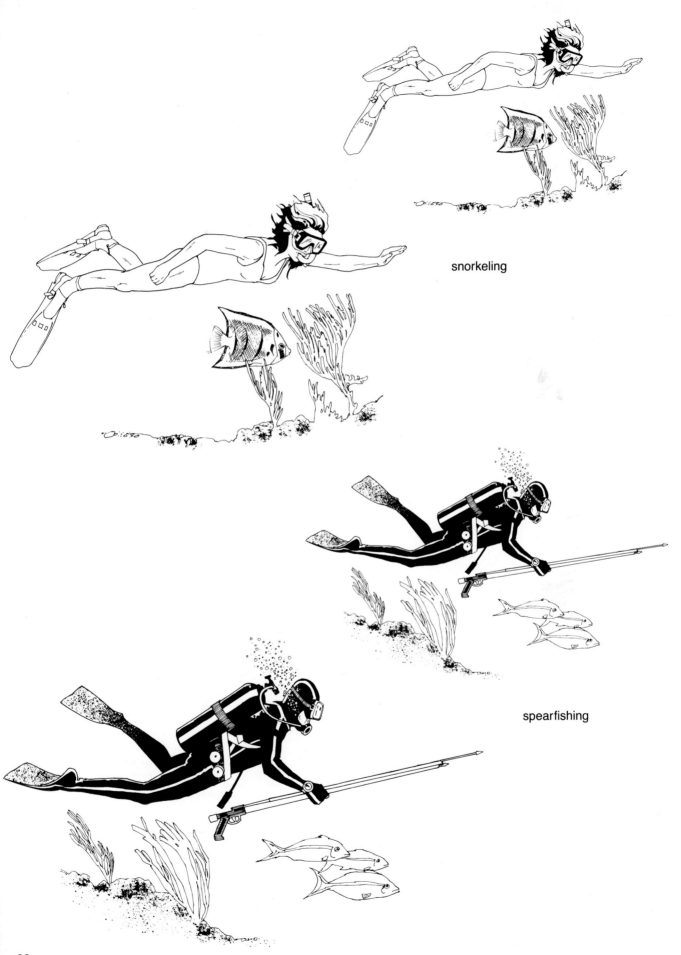

snorkeling

spearfishing

28

scuba diving

snorkeling

scuba diving

waterskiing

surfing

water volleyball

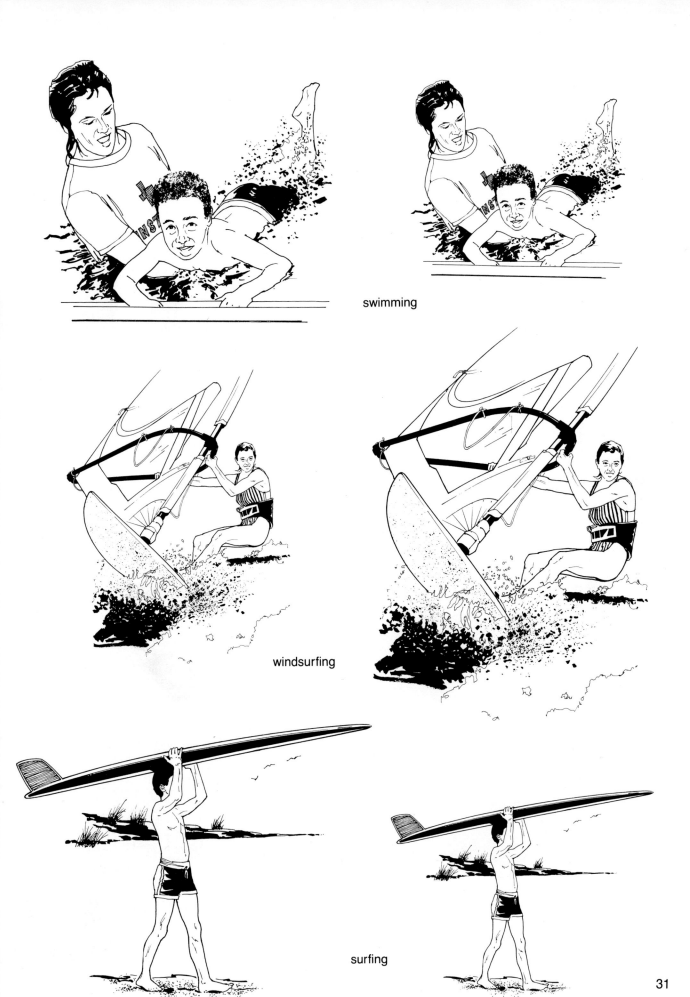

swimming

windsurfing

surfing

surfing

surfing